The Secret Lives of Estheticians

The Secret Lives of Estheticians

MARY NIELSEN

illustrated by Sarah Jensen

SKINTELLIGENT RESOURCES

Portland, Oregon

Illustrations throughout by Sarah Jensen

Photographs used for illustrations © Rene - stock.adobe.com, © Samuel B. - stock.adobe.com, © ysbrandcosijn - stock.adobe.com, © akatz66 - stock.adobe.com, © JJAVA - stock.adobe.com, © biker3 - stock.adobe.com, © everettovrk - stock.adobe.com, © HLPhoto - stock.adobe.com, © paolo maria airenti - stock.adobe.com, © Wolna - stock.adobe.com, © Joseph - stock.adobe.com, © pathdoc - stock.adobe.com, © litts - stock.adobe.com, © Andrey Popov - stock.adobe.com, © Africa Studio - stock.adobe.com, © alexandre zveiger - stock.adobe. com, © Ranta Images - stock.adobe.com, © Kurashova - stock.adobe.com, © AS Photo Project - stock.adobe. com, © Alexander Mak - stock.adobe.com, © Yann Poirier - stock.adobe.com, © tong2530 - stock.adobe.com, © Drobot Dean - stock.adobe.com, © styxclick - stock.adobe.com, © Rasulov - stock.adobe.com, © Artem - stock. adobe.com, © sigma1850 - stock.adobe.com, © LIGHTFIELD STUDIOS - stock.adobe.com, © DragonImages - stock.adobe.com, @CAMINHO_DO_DESPERTAR from nappy.co, @MARK.C from nappy.co

FIRST EDITION

ISBN 10: 0-6921-5618-6

ISBN 13: 978-0-69-215618-6

18 19 20 21 22   CS   10 9 8 7 6 5 4 3 2 1

DEDICATED TO

the skin care professionals who find joy
in transforming skin and lifting the
self esteem of their fellow human beings

CONTENTS

FORWARD

The profession of a skin care therapist is a satisfying one.

We provide treatments using state-of-the-art advanced equipment and requiring a deep, histologic understanding of skin and its interactions with acids, electrical charges, ultrasonic vibrations, hydrotherapy, antioxidants, growth factors, vitamins, enzymes, and more. We also have the honor of providing treatments with a human touch. We interact by touching skin, the human body. We see people at their most vulnerable, making esthetics an intimate and privileged profession.

It's a profession that can have its 'days,' both humorous and poignant. Every day is different—different treatments, different people, and different encounters.

The stories in this book are from the professional careers of some industry leaders in the Pacific Northwest. They are intended to inspire, to amuse, and to encourage sister (and brother) esties in this incredible field. Many of you have had similar experiences and will be able to identify with these stories.

It's our shared experiences that bind us together.

For all stories, names have been changed to protect the innocent.

Beware; for I am fearless, and therefore powerful

- MARY SHELLEY -

HOT DOGS

Randi entered her facial room to find a thirty-something aged man sitting on a stool, hands folded nervously in his lap.

"I really need your help," Montel pleaded, "It's too hard for me to take care of this on my own. I end up cutting myself,"

Randi listened to his request for services and agreed.
"But," she said, "if this gets weird at any time, I'm done,"

Montel agreed.

Montel arrived in a timely fashion for each of his appointments. Randi completed the service efficiently and without incident. Montel and Randi seemed to have developed a rhythm, and things were fine for several visits. Then Montel began to voice dissatisfaction with the service Randi was performing.

"You left it too long," was his complaint after one session.

"It was too short... I itched for weeks," after another.

THE SECRET LIVES OF ESTHETICIANS
MARY NIELSEN

Randi finally convinced Montel to have his balls waxed at his next appointment, rather than the trimming she had been performing regularly.

For his first ball waxing appointment, Montel arrived promptly. Randi left him alone in the treatment room to undress. When she returned, she found him lying on the bed, naked, except for a pair of socks.

"Wow, man! You didn't really have to get this undressed. I only need to see the part I'm waxing," she commented, with some humor in her voice.

Montel was to the point of almost hyperventilation.

"I'm freakin' out!" he cried, "Can I smoke a cigarette?"

"No," Randi asserted, "This is a spa. No smoking here,"

"Well can I do a line of coke?" Montel begged, "It'll relax me,"

"Absolutely not!" Randi spat, "You should have smoked a joint in the car before you came in, if you want to be relaxed,"

She demonstrated the waxing technique to Montel by waxing a small strip of hair on his inner thigh, and he maintained his composure.

"You're right," he took a deep breath, "This isn't so bad."

Randi prepped the skin and applied wax to a small section of Montel's scrotum. She pulled the skin taut and then pulled the tail of the hard wax.

Montel jumped off the facial table and began pacing around the table, yelling, "M*th%rf^cker!"

He ended the service, got dressed, and left.

After work, Randi was out for the evening with her group of friends. As the women enjoyed 'girl time' and a few cocktails, Montel appeared with a tray full of hot dogs. He placed them on the table in front of Randi, and without saying a word, turned and left.

Randi never saw Montel again.

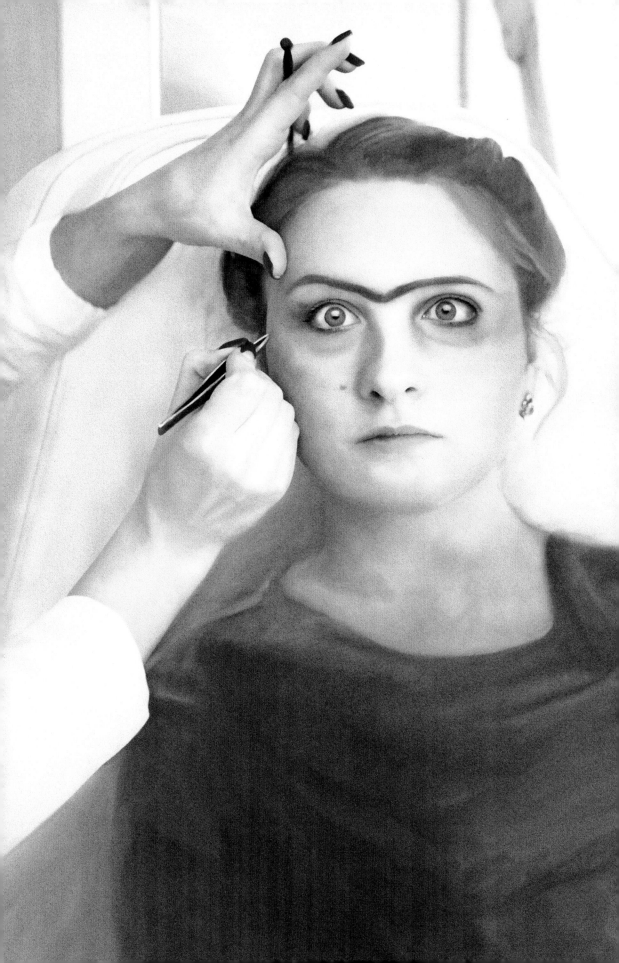

WANT A MINT?

Christine's teenage client was not exactly the most cooperative as she sat in the facial chair, arms crossed rebelliously. She knew it was the client's mother who had made the appointment originally and who now sat in the lounge, waiting patiently for her daughter's unibrow to be removed.

Christine wanted to finish the treatment and return her client back to Mom as soon as possible. She waxed one brow successfully before Babette belched loudly from the chair.

"I need to sit down," Babette said quietly.

Christine looked at her curiously.

"You are sitting down," she replied.

THE SECRET LIVES OF ESTHETICIANS
MARY NIELSEN

Babette inched herself off the facial chair and slid to the floor in a slump, eyes closed. Alarmed, Christine uttered a quick shout to Mom, who rushed in from the waiting room.

"What happened?" Mom asked urgently.

"She isn't feeling well..." Christine answered as she watched Babette come to, wild-eyed and searching around the room. And then, in horror, she watched Babette open her mouth and emit explosive, retching vomit.

Christine sopped up the puke with towels while Babette sat, pale and quiet, in the facial chair once again.

"She can't leave with one brow waxed and one brow furry," Mom whined, "You have to finish."

While Babette sighed deeply with vomit-fragranced breath, Christine finished waxing the other brow.

ZEN BUDDA

Cheryl 'Zen' Miller has tapped the fountain of youth. Her radiant smile and ebullient aura seem to belie her thirty-plus years in fitness and health. Is her 'Budda Butter' the secret?

Zen's naturally curious nature and inner drive to do more and be better has served her well in her career. She began as a fitness instructor, teaching aerobics in the 1980's when all of suburban America was aerobicizing with Jane Fonda. As she led her classes through their routines, Zen wondered about how the muscles worked together to tone and strengthen the body. She took on the adventure of becoming a massage therapist. And continued as a fitness instructor. While working as a massage therapist, she became curious about the skin covering the muscles that she was working on. So she took on the adventure of becoming a licensed esthetician and then a master esthetician. And continued as a fitness instructor and a massage therapist. She incorporated all of these modalities into one business, The Zen Lounge, located in Tacoma, Washington.

The Zen Lounge is a popular destination spa for both facials and massages. Zen has developed her own massage techniques and personally trained her staff. Her morning pilates class is standing room only. It's no wonder The Zen Lounge has been on 'Seattle/Tacoma's Best of List' for years.

60

Zen is an experiential and fearless learner. She began developing her own 'Budda Butter,' a CBD-based massage lotion twenty years ago. Tweaking it to perfection, she would cook it up in her kitchen, package it, and market it to a dozen or more spas across the United States. She casually approached the owner of GlyMed about helping her create a commercial large batch recipe for her 'Budda Butter' and after first declining, GlyMed came back and said yes. Zen worked with chemists to find the perfect balance of slip-and-glide on the skin that could withstand the heat of Arizona or the mugginess of the South.

After participating in the 2017 Skin Games, Zen was honored to be a judge in the 2018 Skin Games. Her years of experience and encouraging spirit make her a thoughtful judge in the Holistic Skincare category.

Zen's latest adventure has her traveling around the United States, teaching her custom facelift facial and massage techniques. She is a popular speaker, giving her all, inspiring new estheticians, and motivating seasoned veterans. Her advice to new skin care professionals is this:

"Set boundaries. Set boundaries in how you spend your time, your energy, and your resources."

This may be something that Zen struggles with herself as she continues to reach for new goals, sharing her 'Budda Butter,' and observing a rigorous training schedule across the country. She is truly an esthetician to admire!

To contact Zen, you can reach her at:
cherylmiller1649@gmail.com

CALL 911

Felicia was thrilled to land her first job. The spa had recently decided to add esthetic services in addition to massage services, and the owner had converted a storage closet into a very tiny facial room. Felicia's easy laugh and Margaux Hemingway smile built an easy rapport with new clients. Despite the minuscule treatment room, her skilled techniques led to re-bookings, and she began to fill her schedule.

One day, Felicia had a couple of hours free between clients, so she decided to spend the time cleaning her little room. She used a rag and a container of wax solvent to vigorously scrub away at the hard-dried wax on her wax pot. It was taking more time and effort than she thought, and she poured a little more solvent onto her rag.

In a split second, a candle flame, burning lightly on a shelf above her, extended itself to the fumes of the wax solvent and traveled like a dart to the wax pot. Suddenly, the wax pot was on fire! In fact, Felicia's hands holding the wax pot were on fire! Felicia took a sharp intake of breath and dropped the wax pot on the floor.

As if things couldn't get worse, the flooring caught on fire! Felicia dropped her gaze to her still flaming hands and stuck them between her legs, quickly extinguishing the fire.

She opened her treatment room door and rushed directly to the reception desk, passing the fire extinguisher along the way.

13

"Call 911!" She cried, "My room is on fire!"

The receptionist calmly stepped around her and grabbed the fire extinguisher. As she dashed to the treatment room to dispense the fire, 911 was alerted by clients in the waiting room.

The fire engine's wailing was heard for blocks before the firefighters actually burst through the door, axes in hand, ready to fight the fire that was already out.

"Please!" the spa owner begged, "There are clients getting massages, and they need peace and quiet!"

The next week, Felicia and the rest of the staff got gifts from the spa owner: electric candles for their treatment rooms.

PS: Felicia earned superficial burns on her hands and on her inner thighs. She is currently healed with no negative effects.

THE SECRET LIVES OF ESTHETICIANS
MARY NIELSEN

You look ridiculous if you dance.

You look ridiculous if

you don't dance.

So you might as well dance.

- GERTRUDE STEIN -

TMI

Portia was a vibrant, charming, seventy-plus-year-old woman who ran a wild animal rescue, "illegally," she whispered. Her arms were full of squirrel bites and raccoon scratches.

She initially came to the med-spa for a series of neck tightening treatments, and at every treatment she insisted on dressing down to nude and wearing a spa gown.

At the last appointment in her series, her esthetician, Carmen, re-entered the treatment room and found Portia standing, rather than lying, on the facial bed, ready for her session.

"I've been thinking," Portia explained, "I've been really happy with my neck tightening," She lifted her leg up on a stool in the room, the spa gown falling away to reveal an aging woman's private area, gray hair and all.

"I'm wondering if I can do some tightening here," She indicated her perineal region.

"We certainly can," Carmen responded and set her up for her first appointment.

At her second appointment, Portia arrived, beaming.

"This really works," she affirmed, "I used my vibrator this morning, and I could really tell a difference."

17

CREEPY GUYS

Every female esthetician will sooner or later experience at least one episode with a 'Creepy Guy.' Here are a few unfortunate tales...

Mallory escorted her male client back to the treatment room and began the facial ritual. The client was quiet as spa music played in the dimly lit room. When she reached the massage portion of the facial, she began the rhythmic hand motions on her client's face, eventually moving down to his shoulders. She paused then, in the dimly lit room, as she saw a 'tent' appear in the sheet blanketing the client during his service.

"Oh, my God, I'm just touching his shoulders."

MORE CREEPY GUYS

Sheila and her co-worker had male clients on their schedules at exactly the same time. Just before their appointments, two 'cool and groovy' guys walked in simultaneously. They were twins, both 50-ish, and wearing identical cargo shorts, Hawaiian shirts, white socks, and Crocs. If their outfits gave no clues, in the treatment room they each bragged profusely about their conquests with women. Bragging soon turned to begging, as they pleaded with Sheila and her co-worker to go out with them, meanwhile bashing their boyfriends, and boasting about their own abilities to satisfy women. Needless to say, Sheila and her co-worker rebuffed all advances. Upon checkout, the two men asked the receptionist for Sheila and her co-worker's personal phone numbers. The receptionist, rightly so, refused.

Sometime later, Sheila was shopping at a local outdoor mall and as she exited a store, she looked up and locked eyes with one of the 'groovy twins.' He was across the courtyard exiting another store, and when he saw her, he began running toward her. Sheila ran. To her car. Locked the door and drove away.

EVEN MORE CREEPY GUYS

Maria opened the letter that arrived in the mail. A newspaper clipping fell out along with a hand-written letter. The newspaper clipping was from a recent open house that her spa had held. Her photo was in the ad, along with other staff. She unfolded the letter and began to read. Her hands began to shake, and she picked up the phone to make an unusual call.

"I'd like to speak to the warden, please." Her voice was shaky. She re-read the letter while she was on hold:

'A friend sent me the newspaper and as soon as I saw your picture, I could tell by the look in your eyes that you wanted me. You're so beautiful. I'll be getting out in three months, and I thought we could start getting to know each other. I know in my heart we are meant to be together. Send me your address so I can come and visit you when I am released.'

Maria sent a copy of the letter to the warden and contacted an attorney. A restraining order was enacted, and Maria never heard from the inmate again.

A FRIEND SENT ME THE
AND AS SOON AS I SAW YOU
I COULD TELL BY THE LOOK
EYES THAT YOU WANTED

YOU ARE SO BEAUTI

I'LL BE GETTING OUT IN
AND I THOUGHT WE COULD S
GETTING TO KNOW EACH OT

I KNOW IN MY HEART
WE ARE MEANT TO BE TO

SEND ME YOUR ADDRESS

SO I CAN COME AND VISIT

YOU WHEN I AM RELEASED.

XO XO XO XO XO XO XO OX

Medi-Spa Staff during their open house

Local Town News

Local Medi-Spa Open
House Smashing Succes

by Sarah Jensen

The scene in front of the medispa on Friday
crowd full of smiles. Everyone in the town enjoyed th
open house that the local medispa had to celebr
month anniversary of its opening. The crowd gathe
everyone got free food and beverages as well as
games. Entertainment was provided by local folk ro
everyone danced late into the night.

Medispa employees took community membe
of the facilities as well as explained the laser pr
medispa recently went through a renovation so th
brand new and ready for life. Plus the spa unve
patient waiting area that is equipped with two la
various magazines, a fountain, and a fish tank w
salt water fish. All in all it seems like a very rela
for a procedure. Lucky community members wer
event with various coupon books for future proc

I'M AN ESTHETICIAN.
WHAT'S YOUR SUPER POWER?

Debora Masten has been one of the most influential people in Oregon in her twenty-year esthetics career. When medical esthetics was in its infancy, she was fortunate enough to have a physician recruit her before she had even been to esthetics school. She got her license and never considered work in a spa setting.

Learning to find the balance in life is a challenge that Debora seems to have overcome. She once resigned from a position at OHSU because it conflicted with her son's sports schedule. By choosing to live a philosophy of 'family first,' Debora has missed the opportunity to work with some amazing people, however she has enjoyed a life that sticks true to her values.

Her medical esthetics career has put her in some unique situations throughout the years. She once performed laser hair removal around a stoma for a client with a colostomy bag. It was rewarding to know that her client would no longer have to have his hair pulled daily when changing the bag. She also took satisfaction once from helping a bride remove her nipple hair before her honeymoon.

One day, Debora thought she had privacy in her treatment room while performing some personal laser hair removal on her bikini area. Her room had skylights, and she noticed a shadow briefly cross the room. Looking up, she saw a team of roofers spying down on her! She skedaddled quickly!

Debora's administrative skills as a boss were tested when a new employee showed up for work with a tiny toilet and put it on the counter. It was labeled 'Tips,' and when a coin was inserted, it made a flushing sound. The new staffer felt Debora was being unreasonable when she asked the toilet be removed.

Debora has an ability to connect with her clients when they are in her treatment room because she's learned to be a sensitive listener. Clients feel open enough to talk about their divorces, affairs, cancer, and other challenging circumstances in life. Her philosophy that people need an ear and not a judge has been the mantra that builds clients' trust.

Debora gets enormous personal satisfaction from building trusting relationships, referring someone to a medical intervention when they have a suspicious lesion, and helping her clients feel better about themselves overall.

Her leadership skills, critical thinking, and commitment to giving back to her profession have allowed her to serve on the Oregon Board of Cosmetology, representing estheticians for several terms as well as serving as an industry expert on many Oregon Rules Advisory Committees. Debora maintains a focus on allowing estheticians to have a broad scope of practice that expands with the introduction of new technology.

With this fulfilling career, she certainly deserves the super hero cape!

MOLE CHECK

The Skinny on Skin is a program promoted by the Melanoma Foundation. It's an online certification for identifying potential cancerous lesions, targeted especially for beauty industry professionals. Most people will see their esthetician or hair dresser more times a year than they see their physician. The Skinny on Skin equips beauty industry pros with the skills needed to bring more awareness to the rise of skin cancer, making this a truly brilliant program.

Find more information at:

https://www.impactmelanoma.org/programs-the-skinny-on-skin

Mandy was a very careful esthetician. Well-practiced and attentive, she approached every treatment with an aim for perfection. As she prepared the room for her next client, she set up her waxing station, ensured the wax temperature was just right, and reassured herself that this treatment was going to go flawlessly. This was her client's second Brazilian waxing session.

When her client arrived, Mandy readily performed the front portion of the wax with ease. As her client was changing position, Mandy noticed a large brown spot on her client's right butt cheek, somewhere between the size of a pencil eraser and a dime.

"Oh," she thought, "I don't remember seeing that mole the last time she was here. Not a problem. I'll avoid waxing over a

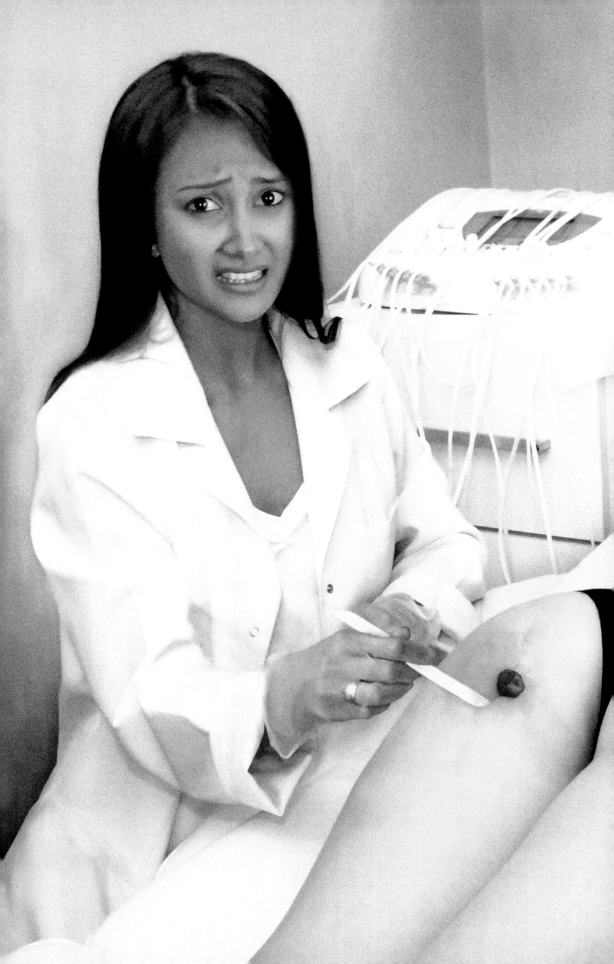

mole, just like I learned in esthetics school,"

However, as she spread the wax, some of it accidentally traveled onto the mole.

"Well, dang it," she thought, "Waxing once over a mole isn't likely to convert any cancerous cells. I'm just going to have to wax over it,"

She prepped the skin, applied the wax, used firm ironing motions to apply the strip, and made a strong pull. She then looked at her client's butt, and the mole was gone!

"Oh no! I've waxed off her mole!" she thought.

Pausing for a split-second to compose herself, Mandy thought about how she was going to tell her client that she had accidentally waxed off her mole, when suddenly she caught a malodorous whiff.

"Oh my! It wasn't a mole..."

She finished the wax in silence.

THE SECRET LIVES OF ESTHETICIANS
MARY NIELSEN

SCHEDULING NIGHTMARE

As an experienced esthetician who has a full book of clientele, it is inevitable that a few scheduling conflicts arise. Thankfully the following circumstances don't occur often...

Paula was a regular client. As a regular client for several years, intimacies were exchanged, and I was privy to the highs and lows of her personal life. I knew that when she started coming to me, she was in the middle of divorce. I listened to the shallow commiserations commonly spouted during divorce proceedings and remained in her confidences as she re-entered the dating world in her late 40's, insecure, and desiring a partner who would not betray her as her ex-husband had done.

I celebrated with Paula as she began dating a man who seemed to be the right fit. He embraced and endeared himself to her college-aged children. They enjoyed the outdoors together, wine tasting, golfing, and shared a love of foreign films. Soon enough, they moved in together.

After about a year, at a regular facial appointment, Paula expressed concern about her personal life.

"Something is happening with Cody," she stressed, "I can't put my finger on it, but he's become distant,"

Julie was another regular client for facial services. As a client for years, she had trusted me enough to share the intimate details of her personal life, much like Paula. She had been single for years, previously divorced, and she was wary about

initiating a relationship with another man, feeling burned by her marriage and prior relationships. She had no children.

One day at a regular facial appointment, Julie exhibited a joyful exuberance that was uncharacteristic, practically floating on the facial bed.

"I've met someone," she eagerly spilled the beans, "I met him at the gym. He's amazing. He's ending a relationship with a real bitch too. His name is Cody,"

My stomach did a flip as I easily connected the dots. My relationship with Paula and Julie was the same; I was their skin care therapist, not their friend or their counselor.

I made sure neither woman was ever scheduled back to back or had to encounter each other in the waiting room. I also honored confidentiality rules and didn't 'rat' one woman out to the other.

These are the real dilemmas of an esthetics practice in a small town...what a scheduling nightmare.

It is *never too late* to be what you *might have been*

- MARY ANNE EVANS -

I'M ON MY PERIOD

"I'm on my period," Samantha's client relayed as she began undressing to prepare for her Brazilian waxing treatment.

Samantha was a newly licensed esthetician and conscientious about doing the right thing in her first job after licensure.

"I'm not sure I'm comfortable waxing that area while you're having your period," Samantha replied, apologetically.

"Please, please!" the client begged, "I've taken the time off work. I've got to have my hair removal today,"

The client climbed on the table and continued her plea, "I can't reschedule. I'm going on vacation. Please!"

Somewhat hesitantly, Samantha prepared her work area and draped her client. As she leaned in for a good visual inspection of the area, she noted that the client had a tampon inserted halfway into her vagina. The end that was sticking out was obviously soggy and soiled.

THE SECRET LIVES OF ESTHETICIANS
MARY NIELSEN

Samantha viewed the scene and told her client, "I'm so sorry, but I'm not comfortable with this. You've got your tampon half-in and half-out, and it's going to be too challenging for me to wax.

I'll have to see you when you get back from vacation," She stepped back.

The client responded by reaching between her legs; in one fell swoop she yanked out the bloody rag of a tampon and flung it across the room.

"No problem. The tampon is gone."

Samantha proceeded to wax.

OUTSIDE THE BOX

Erika Wilson has been thinking outside the box since at least 2004. That is when she introduced esthetics to communities in the Gorge. This rural area of the Pacific Northwest had their doubts about Erika's ability to stay in business longer than a year, but she has proven them wrong with her commitment to people, both clients and staff.

Erika's core values include remaining sensitive to the needs of her clients as individuals. Surrounded by a large array of fancy technology and a full schedule of people with skin issues, practitioners working in esthetics can become less sensitive to their clients over time, forgetting that each individual comes in for a problem that is important and unique to themselves. Appointments can be very emotional, and Erika strives to have each person treated with love and compassion.

One client was a regular and had already had a series of six chemical peels with outstanding results. She was returning for a routine maintenance peel and as Erika began applying the solution, the client complained that this peel felt hotter and more aggressive than the peels from previous series. Erika also noted that the client's skin frosted immediately. She neutralized and removed the peel and while questioning her client in that process, she learned that the client had applied a retinol to her skin the night before. This retinol acted as a booster when reacting with the chemical peel solution, and the client received a much deeper peel than she bargained for. The results were beautiful, luckily, but it taught Erika that the consultation process before a treatment is of utmost importance, even with a long-term client that you think you know.

Even the most difficult and challenging clients really just want their voices heard, and Erika's approach is to remain calm and listen. Let them unload. And don't be afraid to dismiss them from your service if they have unrealistic expectations about treatments.

Erika's thinking outside the box includes taking the time to check on her clients when they don't have time to come to her. A client who was involved in the cherry-picking harvest couldn't come to the office to have Erika check her skin after a procedure. So Erika traveled to her, bringing her the skin care products she needed to keep her skin healthy.

A fourteen-year-old client that Erika treated for acne was so influenced by Erika's help that she approached Erika about working at the med-spa as a part of her Senior Project when she was in high school. This young woman went on to esthetics school and started her own spa upon graduation. When Erika had a staff opening about a year later, she was pleased to offer the position to this passionate skin care professional and was surprised to learn that the young woman's passion was sparked when she began seeing Erika at age fourteen.

As a woman, wife, mom, friend, sister, aunt, grandma, business owner, and skin care professional, it can be overwhelming to balance the roles and the demands on today's esthetician. Erika finds her 'me' time through the social sport of tennis, exercising her athleticism in the process.

Erika's advice to estheticians in practice today is to never stop learning. As this field is constantly changing and evolving, make it a habit to read a journal article, listen to a podcast, or learn something new every day to keep current in the industry.

As a business owner, she takes the time to develop a strong team, and she doesn't hire in haste. She treats her staff like family and recognizes that lots of communication makes a stronger team. Resolve conflicts quickly and don't forget to have fun!

To contact Erika, you can reach her at:
erika@columibalaserskincenter.com

WOW! IT MUST REALLY HURT!

Lisa arrived at the office early so she could perform some personal laser hair removal—her bikini area—before the work day started. She closed the exam room door and got out the ultrasound gel and goggles. She turned on her laser and waited for the device to go through its start-up cycle. The machine chimed its readiness, and Lisa entered the settings for her treatment on the screen. She then moved a stool in front of the laser, hiked up her skirt, and sat down.

Ready. As she lifted her leg to get a good view and proper placement of the handpiece, she had to shift her weight and balance precariously on the stool. She fired.

She rebalanced her weight, shifted again, placed the handpiece and fired.

With her leg bent up in an unnatural yoga pose, ankle close to her neck, balancing on one side of her sit bones, Lisa laughed at herself, thinking about how funny she must look if someone came into the room. She fired again.

THE SECRET LIVES OF ESTHETICIANS
MARY NIELSEN

This time she lost her balance, falling completely off the stool. As she dropped to the floor, the laser handpiece accidentally fired, shooting a hole through her skirt and pulsing into unprepped skin, leaving a burn. Lisa screamed in astonishment.

She assessed her situation on the floor, examining her skirt and determining the burn on her leg to be superficial. She clambered up and turned off the laser. Hair removal session over!

When she left the room, the morning staff was gathered at the desk.

"Wow! Laser hair removal must really hurt!" a co-worker remarked, "We could hear you yelling, and we had no idea it was so noisy,"

Lisa agreed, "It's not pain free."

STINKY FEET

Belinda loved her job. She'd worked at the corporate-owned spa for going on eight years, climbing her way up from facial technician, to lead esthetician, to shift supervisor. For her next role, she was eyeing assistant manager. She managed a team of ten estheticians and did it well, thriving on coaching newly licensed estheticians and watching them build confidence and practical skill sets. When her staff had a high rebooking rate, she was as proud as a mama whose baby just took their first steps.

Robert was one of her protégés. Surprised at how much he loved performing facials, he got personal satisfaction when he could see his clients visibly relax during the service. He loved to improve their skin's condition with a series of microdermabrasions or chemical peels.

This particular day he had taken his client back to the treatment room for a facial, giving her privacy to undress and get on the treatment table. Belinda watched him enter the room to begin the service. A few minutes passed before he exited the room, closing the door softly behind him.

"Bee, there's something wrong with my client," he stated with concern, "She's got an infection or something. I think it's..." Robert made a circular motion with his hands in front of his abdomen, "something to do with her lady parts, if you know what I mean,"

"What makes you say that?" Belinda questioned, "Did she note something on her health history? Did she say something?"

"No," Robert continued, "But the smell. It's so bad. I'm not sure I'm going to be able to do her facial. It's so strong it almost makes me gag. And, it's coming from her, you know, lady area," and again Robert made the circular motion with his hands, "It's really bad,"

"Let's check it out," Belinda replied.

She approached the room and entered quietly. Robert hesitated and stood outside the treatment room door.

A quick assessment was all that she needed. Belinda returned to the hallway.

"Robert. Really. Lady parts? It's her feet. Her feet stink!"

Robert froze in confused horror.

Belinda continued, "You're going to offer her a complimentary upgrade to her facial service. She's going to get a hot towel on her feet and a tea tree oil massage. Now get in there and make it happen!"

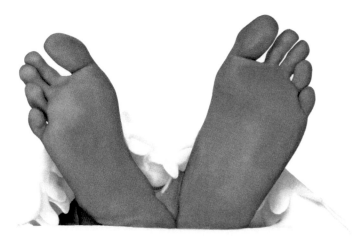

Robert's client was over-the-moon with her facial and complimentary upgrade. She spread the word, and soon Robert was known for starting his facials with a hot towel and tea tree oil foot massage.

Belinda was soon promoted. Not to assistant manager, but esthetic educator for the corporate region.

ANGEL IN OUR MIDST

Annette Scott is a veteran esthetician with a remarkable life story.

It begins in the 1970s, where she worked briefly as a model while waiting tables on the side. Interestingly, she found the behind-the-scenes action more stimulating than the walk down the runway, and so she set her sails on becoming a make-up artist. While working with skin, she fell in love with it and has been a licensed professional ever since. After 31 ongoing years in practice, she has had a full life in esthetics and is an inspiring role model to newer estheticians everywhere.

After getting licensed, Annette opened a spa connected to her house. While raising her daughter as a single mom, she could easily send her child off to school, see clients throughout the day, pick her daughter up from school, and go back to work. Her daughter has great memories of growing up next to Mom's spa.

One great story from this time occurred while performing a Brazilian wax on a soon-to-be bride. Never having been waxed before, the client's pain tolerance was low, and she let out a scream with each pull of the wax. After only halfway through the treatment, the client decided she couldn't take it anymore and asked Annette to stop the service. The bride went off on her honeymoon with a half Brazilian!

In 2011, Annette started the Reflections program at the Celilo

Cancer Center in The Dalles, Oregon. By helping cancer patients deal with the ravaging effects of radiation and chemotherapy on the skin, her care and technique paved the way for blending esthetics with treatments for cancer. She puts her makeup skills to use in assisting these patients, as well as fits them for wigs, scarves, and hats. Her impact on their self-image is immeasurable.

Annette might have invisible wings and an invisible halo in her daily work with cancer patients. She spends time daily with women who have just received devastating news. One woman had received news that her genetic testing was positive, and she was going to have to call her pregnant daughter to let her know she was carrying the genes for cancer. She had another patient who would not undress or get under the sheets for her facial service because she had been sexually abused. Annette is able to cry with her patients and give them support while still performing her work exceptionally. She has learned the subtle body language that lets her know when she has permission to give her patients a hug. She has an extra measure of understanding for these patients.

Annette has some sound advice for new estheticians in the field:

"Give a good facial massage. It's better than any equipment. If you have extra time, give an extra-long massage, add an eye treatment, or walk your client to her car. Work hard. Know your products. Never stop learning. Get oncology trained!"

Annette challenges all estheticians to be the best they can be. By setting the bar higher, we elevate our profession, and by raising our own industry's standards, we get more respect when working with medical professionals. Furthermore, we elevate our standard of living with wages. Thank you, Annette, for the model of care, compassion, and excellence that you are for this industry.

To contact Annette, you can reach her at:
skincarebyas@gmail.com

BEAUTIFUL LIPS

Bonnie, an esthetics instructor, was supervising an esthetic student as she performed a Brazilian wax for the first time. She coached her student through the process, using lots of positive affirmations at every step.

As the student spread the hard wax, Bonnie commented, "Beautiful lip," referencing the tab of wax the student left as a handle to remove the wax.

Several days later, Bonnie was ordering lunch at a small café. The waxing client, a 40-something woman, sat with some friends at a nearby table. She made eye contact with Bonnie, and Bonnie stopped by her table to say hello.

"I just want you to know—you made my day when I was in earlier this week!" the client exclaimed. She turned to her girlfriends, "She told me I have beautiful lips!"

The client interpreted Bonnie's encouragement of her student's waxing technique as a compliment of her own labia majora.

Awkward. Bonnie smiled.

She continues teaching and no longer calls the hard wax handle a 'lip.' She calls it a 'tab.'

47

I had to make my own living
and *my own opportunity.*
But I made it!
Don't sit down and wait for
the opportunities to come.
Get up and make them.

- MADAM C.J. WALKER -

SISTERS FROM ANOTHER MISTER

Samie Patnode, policy analyst, and Cerynthia Murphy, qualification analyst, are powerhouse women who work behind the scenes keeping the enormous government machines of the Oregon Health Licensing Office moving forward. Both women began working for the state of Oregon in 1996. Samie was attracted to working in government because she was raised in a house where her parents often had political discussions and encouraged Samie to have an opinion on the world around her. Cerynthia's love of statistics comes from her father, who would quiz Cerynthia as a child, having her work out math problems in her head as a family game.

These women began on the front lines, in enforcement. Cerynthia started as an Investigation Liaison, responsible for coordinating scheduling with investigators. Both credit their longevity, rising the ranks of the Health Licensing Office, to their intelligence and political savvy. They have seen leaders in the agency come and go along with Oregon law changes. They have seen public perceptions and social awareness change. As their responsibilities have shifted and grown, they have always managed to have roles that require an interaction and dependence on the other. Nowadays, they have worked together for so long they often finish each other's sentences during interviews and are quick to complement the strengths of their working relationship. A genuine respect and affection for each other is apparent.

The Oregon Health Licensing Office is responsible for the scope of practice of sixteen different professional industries: hearing aids, nursing homes, hairdressers, estheticians, barbers, nail techs, athletic trainers, midwives, denturists, body art practitioners, and finally, sex offender treatment. Each board has a meeting schedule and agendas to fulfill. Scope of practice issues, collaborations with other state agencies, like the Higher Education Coordinating Commission, public hearings, and research fill their time readily.

Cerynthia can reflect on her twenty-two years of service with a sense of pride. Her dedication ensured that individuals who work in a particular industry are competent and demonstrate the skills to succeed. Her work has led directly to protecting the public on various fronts: the development of a diversion program for respiratory therapists, as well as an initiative for body piercing and tattooing education, including an examination for certification at a time that led the country.

Cerynthia has been directly responsible for the Health Licensing Office having cosmetology exams translated into a number of different languages to serve a more diverse workforce in the state. She works hard to get 'buy-in' from the larger groups that she works with, like individual cosmetology schools. Her strengths include her heart to see each person coming in to the office as an individual with their own story. She wants to do her part to help them succeed in their profession.

In Samie's role as a policy analyst, she has learned to read with a legal lens to interpret legislative intent. This has challenged her to think outside the box to find solutions to problems. She has to often work for years to see ideas come to fruition, and has witnessed the scope of practice in esthetics especially morph dramatically. Esthetics in Oregon was once called Facial Technology, and estheticians were allowed to work on the face only, to the 7th vertebrae of the body. It took over ten years from the first discussions, for the legislation that finally enacted the second tier of esthetics licensure, Certified Advanced Esthetics, to become reality. Samie's organization and leadership skills get her involved in other divisions within the office, working collaboratively and creating greater efficiencies for the government.

These women have taken on the birth of new professional licensure certifications, like Body Art Practitioners, Midwifery, and Polysomnography. These professions have been wrought with political overtones that often have strong emotional inferences. Midwifery is one example; everyone has an opinion on home births.

Samie and Cerynthia admit to times of disagreement throughout the years, however they describe it as an argument between sisters. They laugh uproariously about an intense period of time when public hearings, agency meetings, long hours, and a misunderstanding about who was responsible for completing a report led to a yelling match where the 'F bomb' was used liberally. They believed they were alone in the office and were mortified to discover that a meeting was being held in another room where their loud conversation was overheard by a large crowd.

Samie and Cerynthia have survived a minefield of office politics, including the time their office was interrupted by state police removing the office leadership. Samie calmly continued the board meeting that was scheduled that day. Business as usual.

Both women work hard to communicate a consistent message to the professional bodies they work to represent. They speak in layman's terms, translating the legalese of complicated legislative language for the professionals they serve.

When asked about how they balance professional and personal lives, Samie laughs.

"Good friends, good wine, and good food!"

Cerynthia heartily agrees. Both admit to not being able to completely tune out the Health Licensing Office when off the clock, but they cope by leaving themselves voicemails or sending themselves emails on weekends and evenings, so they can take care of it when they return to the office.

Samie and Cerynthia find the humor in rough situations and clearly have found a groove working together that benefits the licensed professionals of Oregon state. These 'sisters from another mister' offer this advice to newbies in esthetics: Be engaged. Get involved. Have a voice. Learn how your government works. And take responsibility.

The professional estheticians of Oregon thank them for their dedication!

MAKE THE APPOINTMENT BEFORE LUNCH

My client was running a few minutes late, but I had the treatment room ready for her. She had booked a ninety minute Consummate Facial, our most relaxing treatment. I was ready to pull out all the stops for her: soft acoustic spa music, candles, aromatherapy, steam, extra massage, paraffin hand and foot mitts.

When she arrived, I led her to the treatment room and showed her where she could put her belongings. I handed her a terry fleece gown and instructed her to put it on and lie down on the heated treatment table, face up. Then I stepped out, mentally reviewing the steps I was about to perform to give her an exceptional facial experience.

As I re-entered the facial room, I closed the door behind me.

"You've got my complete attention for the next 80 minutes," I said soothingly.

I repositioned the sheet and coverlet over her body, making her feel secure. Then I stood at the foot of the bed and lightly held her feet. I moved to the head of the bed next and began the cleansing ritual, wrapping her head in a warm towel. I had her take several deep breaths, exhaling and mentally letting go of tension and stress so she could fully sink in and enjoy the facial.

As I cleansed her face, I noticed her body stiffen slightly. Regardless, I proceeded with the steps of the facial, double cleansing followed by a light exfoliating mask with steam. While the steam worked its magic, I performed a foot massage and then applied paraffin booties. Same with her hands. As I turned off the steam and began to remove the enzyme, I could see her stomach muscles flexing, and she began to squirm slightly, repositioning herself on the facial table. I waited until she resettled and then continued to the facial massage phase of treatment.

As I worked her décolleté and shoulders, she whispered, "I'm sorry, but I must have eaten something that didn't agree with me for lunch. I'm going to have to pass gas,"

"Of course," I whispered back, "I totally understand,"

I pulled my hands off her face, giving her inaudible permission to fart.

A loud 'BLAHHHTT' escaped into the room with an accompanying foul aroma.

"Oooooooh! That wasn't gas!" my client exclaimed.

She grabbed the sheet underneath her as well as the sheet and coverlet on top of her and pulled them up in a diaper-like fashion between her legs. Like a bunny on steroids, she bounded off the treatment table, grabbing her purse and clothing in one huge motion. She then skip-hopped out the door and out of the office, holding her ginormous diaper between her legs with one hand.

I sat for a moment to absorb the speed of the events and then belly-laughed out loud.

My client was gone. I was new at this and didn't really know how to handle the situation. I didn't reach out to my client, and I didn't hear from her.

Three years went by when the phone rang.

"Hello. This is Sheryl Smith. You might not remember me, but I'd like to make an appointment,"

"Hi Sheryl. Yes, I remember you. Let's make an appointment for before lunch."

UNEXPECTED REWARDS

My new client, Kate, was a prominent member of the town's upper crust. A community matriarch, she had immensely more disposable income than I did. She was also known to be a long-term client at a well-established facial salon, and I was delighted that she had made an appointment for a facial with me at my own med-spa. It was going to be a feather in my cap if I could recruit her business; I knew my appointments would increase if she was pleased with my service, and her word-of-mouth referrals would be an important marketing move for me.

She was a short, stocky woman, well known for her bleached blond long hair at an age when most women had at least hints of gray. She loved obviously false lashes, jewel-colored eyeshadow, bright colors, and wearing hats with matching shoes and purses. She was a community leader in many areas, her family guaranteed to fill tables at every charity dinner for every imaginable cause: women's shelters, dog rescues, local theatres, school sports. You name it, the family kept things running in town. She kept all the balls in the air, hosting teas and luncheons to raise awareness for endangered species, community college art fairs, and more. She was charismatic, used to getting her way, and her personality filled a room effortlessly.

I had carefully prepared the facial treatment room for her visit, making sure everything was perfect to make the best first impression.

She blew into the waiting room in a grand way, deep pink Jackie O hat, matching purse and pumps. I greeted her warmly, escorting her down the hall and into the dimly lit treatment room. I indicated the chair and area for her to place her things.

She plopped her purse down and yanked off her hat, turning to me, "Do you mind if I take off my wig?" and without waiting for my reply, she pulled her wig off her head and placed it on the lampshade.

There she stood, bald as an egg. I'm sure my eyes widened as I tried to stop my mouth from falling open.

I left the room to give her privacy to put on her spa gown. Upon my return, she was settled nicely into the facial bed. In her spa gown, she seemed tinier and frailer than she had in her couture suit a few minutes before.

THE SECRET LIVES OF ESTHETICIANS
MARY NIELSEN

I began the facial experience. With dim lighting, quiet spa music, and the connection of human touch, I felt Kate's armor gently fall away and her body relax into the bed. Soon enough, tears began to flow silently down the sides of her face onto the towel beneath her head. Occasionally, she would emote a tiny shudder as she cried. I continued performing the steps of the facial without saying a word, deciding that since this was our first personal encounter, I'd let her initiate the conversation when she was ready.

Eventually, she said softly, "I'm so tired. I'm carrying so much, and I'm so tired,"

Slowly, she shared that she had terminal cancer. She was secretly getting treatments out of town, not feeling as if she could reveal that kind of information to anyone. She couldn't bear to be the subject of town gossip. She also couldn't see her regular esthetician because she didn't trust her confidentiality. She was worried about her husband, her children, and her grandchildren's ability to manage the family dynamics without her vitality and guidance. She fretted about the numerous charities that she supported and how they would continue without her influence.

She was right. She was carrying a lot.

The facial was finished and when she exited the treatment room, her persona was in place again; strong, driven family matriarch.

Kate died in her sleep several weeks after her appointment with me. I never told anyone she had been my client. I didn't reap the benefits of a word-of-mouth referral from her. My appointment book didn't fill up.

But, I consider the privilege of letting her be vulnerable and giving her personal attention and human touch an immeasurable gift and one of the most satisfying reasons for continuing in this profession.

ABOUT THE AUTHOR

A technician, educator, mentor, and business owner, Mary Nielsen has been at the forefront of medical esthetics since its infancy in the early 1990s. She is currently Vice Chair and Industry Expert on the Oregon Board of Certified Advanced Estheticians. She is the author of A Compendium for Advanced Aesthetics, a Guide for the Master Esthetician. She is a contributor to Milady Standard Esthetics: Fundamentals, Edition 12 and writes regularly for Milady Pro.

She is the Executive Director of Spectrum Advanced Aesthetics, the founder of the Cascade Aesthetic Alliance as well as the creator of Skintelligent Resources.

To contact Mary, you can reach her at:
mary@spectrumlasertraining.com

Made in the USA
Columbia, SC
29 September 2018